T0303428

SANDSTORM

Anas Hassan

Sandstorm

B
G S
P

First published in 2021
Eyewear Poetry, an imprint of
Eyewear Publishing Limited, The Black Spring Press Group
Grantully Road, Maida Vale, London W9,
United Kingdom

Typeset with graphic design by Edwin Smet

ISBN 978-1-913606-74-9

BLACKSPRINGPRESSGROUP.COM

ANAS HASSAN

studied history and international relations at Downing College, Cambridge. He is an experienced strategy consultant and business mentor, has run several marathons and ultramarathons, and lives in London. His pamphlet, *'Bibi, Are You Living?'* was published by Eyewear Publishing in 2017, and his work has appeared in a number of poetry magazines and journals. His poems featured in an exhibition of poetry and art on the theme of memory, held at the Menier Gallery in London in 2019 in collaboration with The Art Cooperative, a group of artists and sculptors. He has performed at venues including the Vortex in Dalston (London Jazz Festival), the Windmill in Brixton and the Poetry Café in Covent Garden.

TABLE OF CONTENTS

GO TO THE RISING SUN, FOR I AM SETTING

WITNESSES

O Yasir, O Sumayyah,
you have a certain
appointment at al-Kawthar –

a reunion more prized than
a herd of red camels or
an Uhud of gold or diamonds.

You taught us we can't walk in snow
without leaving a trace behind.

'BIBI, ARE YOU LIVING?'

When the snoring stopped
as you perched by the fire

with loving impudence you asked:
'Bibi, are you living?'

You listened awestruck to your Scheherazade,
convoluted ancestral tales

repeatedly embellished: tales of
Salim and Anarkali, Layla and Majnun,

the knighted poet of the East,
the Bollywood tragedy king.

There you sat, coiled mischievously,
sipping hot salty tea by the Arabian shore.

You called the tea green,
though it was dark brown as the Thames.

And now, you crave it on the ward,
though they don't have it here, of course.

Your shallow intermittent breaths keep me vigilant
in uneasy silence.

LAST WORDS

Go to the rising sun,   for I am setting

We are on the line of position 157-33
We are running North and South

Open the shutters
I want the sunlight to greet me
I don't want to go home in the dark

Do not disturb my circles

It is better to be a crystal and be broken, than to remain perfect like a tile on a housetop

That's article ninety-eight;   now go on to the next

Do I look all right? Give me my brush and my makeup

Already my foot is in the stirrup

Too late for fruit,   too soon for flowers

          Look how the sun lights the trees!

I seem to have been only like a boy, playing on the seashore,
and diverting myself, now and then, in finding a smoother pebble,
or a prettier shell

Do you know   where the apothecary lives?

A certain butterfly   is already   on the   wing

YELLOW ROSE

You're strapped tight, waiting for home,
like you waited for your father
to come back from the factory,
and from his other family;

like you waited for your classmate's letter
during a summer break in the hills:
she expressly wrote, 'No visitors.
Don't try to find me, it's no use.'

You thought you saw her again
as you looked out the window
at a yellow rose swaying in the breeze.

A young mother steps in at the bakery on Chinbrook Road
as you try to buy a thick-sliced white loaf:
'They don't understand the Queen's English around here!'
She knows how hard it is to keep going
in a place you never expected to call home:
concrete for mountains, buses for horses, tarmac for rivers.

You ring the bell for servants
you had to let go years ago,
along with a Damascus blade,
first edition of Hafez,
the matchstick Houses of Parliament
your father brought back from London
for your fifth birthday.

Your breath is laboured.
You want to feel the last glow of the sun.
It's almost midnight.

FATHER'S DAY

I'm looking for some shears to cut back the ivy.
Among fragile textbooks and grimy garden tools
I spot a terrace of stumps and a ball –
dull and scratched, once-golden lettering faded.
I knock the stumps in by the apple tree
like we used to, pause at the end of my mark,
and speed to the crease through a gap in the rose bushes.

You're standing at the gate, smiling,
a copy of *The Times* under your arm.
I picture a crescent and star tattoo on your left wrist
(strange to think of you with a tattoo).
Now the detached house is a block of flats,
cloaking our makeshift Lord's in shade.

I really should take your books back to the library:
The Wisdom of Father Brown,
The Power of Positive Thinking,
How to Win Friends and Influence People,
Wisden Cricketers' Almanack 1955.

I'm not sure what I'll say when I see you,
except talk of biology tests and failed experiments.
Maybe we'll watch *Going for Gold*
while you work your way through drab potatoes
and mushy carrots, and the rice pudding gets cold.

The doorbell rings.
A sheepish boy dressed in gleaming white
wants to look for the ball he's lost through a gap
in the wall somewhere.

Maybe behind the peach tree.

LAST INNINGS

Stumps shattered.

Arms aloft.

Smile triumphant.

I should have served up

half volleys and

long hops

not searing

rib-lashing bouncers.

I thought only of victory.

I see him now, quietly peeling off his pads

shuffling out of the gloom

into the pavilion-conservatory for the last time.

ASHES

At ten I wanted to win the Ashes
but grassed a torrent of crucial catches.

At twenty I craved a gold statuette
but auditions put me in a cold sweat.

At thirty I set sights on Parliament
but couldn't prevail in an argument.

At forty I spied a spot on the board
but profits dived and my job went offshore.

At fifty I scoured Chelsea property
but overlooked a disused cemetery.

At sixty I've jilted all ambition
except for dodging Moat, the mortician.

DOUBLE LATIN

When you swept off for good
with your not-yet-in-vogue-again satchel
and battered bike,
Tuesday afternoons became
doodled purgatory, declined
in the pluperfect subjunctive.

It wasn't just Iceni and Helvetii
in the Lower Fifth that Lent Term.
Sniggering schoolboys found laughs in Tacitus
that seasoned scholars would toil to unearth
as the Freemantle Doctor breezed through
the cricket coliseum
and knocked Agricola off his feet.

On the desk in your new digs:
a sweater charged with lions
from a former pupil who plays the part
I once cast for myself.

SEPIA WINTER

You're planted in December snow
in a Mary Quant dress
(that mattered then),
carrying a half-smiling boy,
always four years old,
as he tries to grab his shiny red Mini.

Musty pages peel away your mask
like bitter kumquat skins stripped
during mid-afternoon repeats
of *Pointless* and *Homes by the Sea*.

An impish girl in nurse's uniform,
straw hat and ribbons,
poses by the ruined aviary
while a watchful friend holds your violin,
on its way to being lost again,
on the 8.17am to Streatham.

Last Christmas you planted a yew tree
at the end of the garden. I'm there now,
in a wicker chair, hunting the wintry sun
under a blanket, shivering.

LOOKING FOR LOUISA

I want to ask about photos I found in the attic.
A girl of five or six in a nurse's uniform smiles,

not reluctantly for once, wraps an arm
around a young cowboy's shoulder.

Our annual pilgrimage – Bath, Chawton, Winchester.
I ask why you won't go to Box Hill.

It reminds you of '65, you say; a dog-ravaged tennis ball,
drowning in a stream, breaks up a late summer picnic.

We trudge along the dark, blustery Cobb.
I want to ask about missing photos of your twenty-first birthday,

about a boy who pretends to sleep
while you read *The Happy Prince* one more time,

and why you planted white daffodils by the back fence.
You say you have to finish *Persuasion* before sunrise.

PERSIAN ROSE

I climb a steep hill in fading light
to reach a secluded house
shielded by willow trees.

I heave open a Chinese lacquer chest:
khaki 1947 ration book,
Sydenham hospital bracelet
(is this where you spent your eighth birthday?),
showjumping rosette pinned to velvet riding hat.

In a corner, long-neglected books
scattered on a Seirafian rug:

a paperback from Luzac & Co, Great Russell Street:
A Brief Narrative of Recent Events in Persia
followed by a translation of
'The Four Pillars of the Persian Constitution' (1909)

and a surprisingly unweathered copy
of *Samson Agonistes* –
you wrote your name, date and form
in neat blue-black ink on the inside cover,
and underlined three lines in thick pencil:

'…apt words have power to swage
The tumours of a troubl'd mind,
And are as balm to fester'd wounds.'

I rummage through the lacquer chest:
a creased theatre programme, Christmas '81,
Toad of Toad Hall at the Old Vic;
half-empty bottles of nystatin, albumin, calcium;

scent of Persian Rose;
a twenty-first birthday card
playing jaunty music with every turn
of a frail silver key.

A framed photo stands orphaned
on a grand piano.
You're in the garden of 5 Chinbrook Road
before the Edwardian house was knocked down.
I think you're around seven years old
(slightly older perhaps),
your brother obliquely at your side.
You're the soldier this time,
hands rammed behind your back.

I wish I could ask what you were thinking,
about the games you played,
what you had for tea,
why you never told anyone
how you fell into the stream.

I see a half-smile, I think,
the same expression I caught
as you leaned forward,
and breathed out, gently,
like water emptying from a pitcher,
that Thursday night last August,
just before midnight.

I hope you can feel the warmth of the sun
and smell sweet musk in the garden.

I hear dogs barking,
a key turning in the latch.

I tilt a step on the Grand Staircase,
and enter an old priest hole.
Imprisoned, shut up from outward light,
I hold my breath and wait.

CEMETERY

I'm here on rocky ground, where I once stood
agape and numb beside the snow-packed road,
the silent crèche of amputated wood,
my cramped cell planted where the old stream flowed,
my new home coated with white sandalwood,
my weary neighbours watchful, spirits bowed,
our rest disturbed by strangers' blazing light
unearthing, excavating through the night.

CHRISTMAS AT HOME

The icy road aborts my escape to the hills.
You bolt the door, draw the curtains,
block the late afternoon sun.
I slump by the fire as you stare at re-runs
of *It Ain't Half Hot Mum* and *George and Mildred*,
and slurp tea from a chipped mug they doled out
on your last day at the mine.

A BIRTHDAY POEM

The cab driver seems perplexed I want to get out here,
leaves me to fight deep November snow to reach the farmhouse.

37 million minutes.

The Pardoner's Tale, due 12th October 1964.
Curiously extensive blue-black ink in the margins.

The Three Musketeers – who is d'Artagnan after Douglas Fairbanks,
a Christmas Eve playmate branded as she leaps off a tattered sofa?

The Catcher in the Rye – don't play by the rules,
escape phonies in a fading imperial city, head for fourteeners and the plains

A snow-white kitten cradled from frost under an apple tree.
Antique mirror, handcrafted, initials scratched on walnut backing.

In the back yard, rocking in a wicker chair by the ancient juniper tree,
you sing Civil War songs, puff on a *Cohiba*,

hear stories of '48: Bradman's Invincibles, the Comeback King
beating Dewey (and the odds) in stoppage time.

613,608 hours.

I leave a music box on the kitchen table: late Victorian,
topaz-coloured, picked up Sunday afternoon from Portobello market,

anachronistically playing 'Thunder on the Mountain'
and 'Tangled Up in Blue' slightly out of tune.

I look down, rugby boots crunching studs in snow,
faded red blazer, 1st XV colours, mud-grazed knees.

25,567 days.

Trudge up the winding Sugar Loaf Road
in fading light to catch a bus home.

TWO STORM WOOD

You told me you loved hills and mud
and Donne, and Arab horses
and pavlova and hot curries laced with chillies.
You untangled your family tree
and made me love Fountains Fell and Moudy Mea.

It was on your birthday that we ran to Two Storm Wood
where you left me, saying I should turn back.
Today is your birthday.

BAKED ALASKA

O the flesh is hot but the heart is cold, you'll be alone when you are old, his favorite country song—on repeat—is being piped through the palace. – 'Baked Alaska, a Theory of', Matthea Harvey

In the sizzling summer of '76 I fell in love,
imitating Master Blaster's Antiguan swagger
and the icy violence of Whispering Death
in the barren gasholder's shadow.

I was munching on sweet green apples,
cooling myself under a swaying hose,
when you enticed me to hot flesh and cold hearts
in the sweltering heat of Orange Pekoe.

One dream remains unmelted –
to hunt down a Baked Alaska worthy of its name.

AS THOUGH WE WERE STRANGERS

You've slipped into the mist of commuters
rushing to catch the Christmas lights

but I've caught your withering half-smile,
just as it was on that New Year's Eve.

Back home, I unlock the trunk
salvaged from an immigrant voyage.

The fire obliterates your letters.
I own your half-smile now.

THE LAST RIDE

Two years since we cut short
our poetic pilgrimage to the Lakes.
Why did we feel so ill at ease?
Was it the damp? The dilapidated cottage?
Next year Chester, we said, or York,
maybe even Andalusia.

After lunch – did we have lunch? –
we grabbed an overnight bag
and set off for Hardy Ward,
on the seventh floor, as I recall.
You would have liked Bronte.
You told me to bring your keys,
said you'd make potato balls
and chocolate eclairs
and we'd watch the race
when you got home.
Next morning they told me you vomited
Zamzam I brought back from Makkah.
I knew I'd have to sit on our brick wall
and watch the bikes fly by on my own.

FLOWER OF KENT

A vast and trunkless leg of wood remains,
an Ozymandias, its former empire
colonised by charlock and groundsel.

You tried to warn me of the woodpecker's raids.
Maybe I thought the ancient tree would last forever.
I didn't notice the slow decline,

each autumn a little less fruit
for the fishmonger who drank cold tea
with three sugars every afternoon at four.

No more home-made apple juice
or rhubarb and apple crumble. You always said
I should pay more attention to genealogy.

I've planted quince by the back fence.
If I can guard against codling moths and brown rot,
perhaps I'll try your recipe for crème brûlée at last.

RELICS OF A NOT-UNCHEQUERED PAST

MERTON PRIORY

My new 24-hour supermarket stands on the foundations of the Chapter House between the disused water mill and the farm by the pond on Maera's homestead. Canons once gathered here to listen to chapters from Augustine's Rule; John stopped by on the way to confront his barons at Runnymede; and a mad incompetent boy was crowned on his sixteenth birthday.

Beneath the car park where I left my Nissan Qashqai SUV stands the church where the black-coped hooded monks spent their days in prayer, beginning at two in the morning and ending at eight in the night.

The TV and DVD aisle, I heard, was where a young man spoke for the first time and a woman carried in a litter began to recover her strength an hour after Compline on the Vigil of the Festival of Bartholomew.

Behind the counter where the fishmonger is gutting and scaling a rainbow trout lies the Scriptorium where Thomas Becket spent hours copying manuscripts from the age of ten and where Walter, father of English universities, learned embrothering in a fair hand.

After three o'clock services, the canons took their exercise in cloisters between the bakery and the organic section before piling on calories at Collation and swilling home-brew.

I just keep from spilling my strong Tanzanian coffee as a boisterous five-year-old runs past, between aisles of tombs.

MAIDEN QUEEN

I'm supposed to sell bespoke, handmade furniture
on a spot where it's said King Charles visited Nell
after the Restoration.

I spend most of my time reading
Sartre and Camus, and writing
badly scanned poetry.

Just after lunch a lady wrapped in black arrives,
lands in an off-white leather chair, swivels to face
a mirrored wall, and stares ahead.

Who is she, and why is she here?

Oksana, Russian countess, newly divorced,
forced to move out of her penthouse apartment
and surrender her private yacht.

Clarissa, weighing up how to tell her parents
she is about to swap a third year at Bart's
for drama school.

Farah, grand-daughter of an exiled
Iraqi diplomat who fought with Faisal
to defy the retreating Ottomans.

Aoife, descendent of goat-herders,
about to split up with the lawyer fiancé
she met at school in Connemara.

The phone rings. Before I can answer,
the chair swivels round, the lady in black stands up,
and walks out into the late afternoon sun.

WHO STOLE THE HYMN BOOKS?

I climb aboard the open platform
of the red double-decker number 15
by the Tower with a troop of tourists
carrying oversized rucksacks
and redundant umbrellas.
Soon their guide valiantly summons Jack Cade
from the street where candlewrights toiled
and where (he says)
Brutus brought his stone back from Troy
and where (he doesn't say)
my father once laboured
opposite the train station
between Salters' Hall Court
and St Swithin's Lane
in a narrow warehouse
crammed with pads, bats, gloves,
leather footballs, feather shuttlecocks.

We crawl round St Paul's,
past Whitefriars Street
where prostitutes and criminals roamed
on the site of a Carmelite priory,
past pop-up food courts
catering to hedge fund managers
where Dickens and Thackeray loitered
in the hope of a meagre advance.
The conductor arrives, his Gibson A14 machine
spewing soon to be discarded tickets
as we pass a large crowd
milling outside the Royal Courts of Justice.
I get off at Charing Cross,
opposite the police station on Agar Street

where the Duke of Sussex laid the foundation stone
of Doctor Golding's Hospital and Medical School
almost two centuries ago.

I wander through a gilded souk,
Belgian chocolate piled into pyramids,
Benjamin Pollock's old shop jammed
with Victorian toy theatres and music boxes.
I watch two students lazily wheel a coffee cart
across the cobbles, avoiding loitering pigeons,
mechanical tourist traps and school parties,
waves of fluorescent jackets grappling with clipboards
almost half their size.

A Cockney flower girl clutches violets and tulips
gathered from the Dutch Resistance,
while her neighbours look on from the Actors' churchyard:
Thomas Arne, composer of *Tom Thumb* and *Rule Britannia*;
Claude Duval, notorious highwayman hanged at Tyburn
to the dismay of his many female admirers;
John Thomas, auctioneer of King Street, dead in January 1831 aged 33.

By the Tin Shed a market porter,
wide rimmed glasses and dangling cigar,
in grimy overalls, stands hands in pockets,
propping himself against a fruit cart.
Fruit and veg salesmen Morris, Frank and Ken
gather in Bedford Chambers,
not yet a glass temple for consumers
stampeding for the latest iPad or iPhone
at the Genius Bar. Morris covers his mouth
with his phone, hat worn at a crooked angle,
Edward G Robinson in *Little Caesar* or *Key Largo*.

George has spotted me.
He has something on his mind.
We drink bitter Arab coffee,
he slips in his confession
as we talk of fêtes and open days,
tulips and forest pansies.
He was the one who stole the hymn books
on the night of the Great Storm.

SEVEN DAYS IN RICHMOND

I

As I jog through Old Deer Park in the morning mist on my way to the lab, a brocket peers from behind a blackthorn tree. I name him Elmer, imagine him descended from Saxon nobility. He watches warily as I head to the plantation.

II

I slip into the Old Library, settle into an Edwardian mahogany armchair upholstered with scenes from the cave at Lascaux, and sip mint tea under a portrait of Sir Thomas Roe, privy councillor, ambassador and drinking partner to Emperor Jahangir at Agra.

III

A birthday present from Martha arrives – a reproduction of the Stag Hunt mosaic of Alexander from the House of the Abduction of Helen at Pella.

IV

I trawl through antique shops near Buckfast Abbey and pick out a leaping stag weathervane in copper, and a mounted skull finished with silvery wire antlers.

V

I spend the afternoon avoiding a murder mystery party that's just checked in. I watch re-runs of *Crimes of the Hart* and read the first thirty pages of *The Wild Red Deer of Exmoor: a digression on the logic, ethics and economics of stag-hunting in England.*

VI

I sunbathe in the garden of the refurbished Stag and Lion, try to block out Mansfield fans celebrating a Cup Final golden goal.

VII

I urge myself to run faster, afraid of being trapped when the culling starts. As I reach the end of the path, a brocket skull, impaled on a bolted iron gate, stares through the winter fog.

HONEYMOON

I had my heart set on the Maldives
but you forced a change of plan.
'It will remind you of your old college,' you said.
So we stayed in the Regency Suite
overlooking the Royal Estate.
Designed for the most discerning of guests:
sophistication, discretion, a personal attendant
eager to meet any request with elegance and tact,
for twenty thousand a night.
But I can't get the rotten sweet smell
of the dead house out of my mind.
Autopsy tables, embalming fluid, bone saws.
In the operating theatre the quickest surgeons
perform amputations in less than a minute.

EARTH, ROCK, SEA
THE ROAD TO SKIBBEREEN

I

Trek for two hours through druidic rocks,
sugar stealers, rows of lime, yew
and Spanish chestnut trees
to megalithic portal dolmen
on the banks of the Martin,
navigate slippery Wishing Steps
between ice house and disused limekiln,
wade through caves
said to be home to elves and goblins,
crouch, hands and knees in wet mud,
reach the Lia Fail at last,
the pillow of Jacob brought to the island by Jeremiah,
(instead I've touched the black stone
Jacob's grandfather set by Adam's altar
in the eastern corner of the Ancient House),
watch friends breathe in powers that a witch,
saved from drowning, supposedly revealed
to the King of Munster.

II

Take a ferry to an island the size of Manhattan,
run past Ardaragh Wedge Tomb
to a hilltop with views of Lonehort Harbour
where General Carew landed
to launch an assault on Dunboy in 1602,
etch windmills on Barleycove sand,
trace the North Atlantic Way
to Mizen Head's lighthouse,
travel on narrow lanes,

articulated lorries exceeding the speed limit,
a horse and carriage carrying a bride
to a church that never seems to appear,
leave Priest's Leap and the Old Forge,
pass Bernadette kneeling in prayer,
fall asleep, finally arrive long after midnight
in the louring shadow of Hungry Hill.

III

Five hours on *The Duchess of Malfi*.
I sit alone, subdued, almost oblivious
to passengers darting side to side
to catch glimpses of dolphins
teasing our battered boat,
seals and harbour porpoises
sheltering in the distance.
I'm badly prepared –
no sunglasses or hat to shield the sun's glare,
no waterproof to keep out pelting rain.
I watch the burly captain heat a mug of coffee
while his wife watches for whales.

I've taken an irrational dislike
to our Charles Marlow,
who hoards his warm coffee,
and leaves me freezing in the evening air.

IV

We climb Knockomagh,
a crooked hill overlooking
Lough Hyne's saltwater lake,
pausing for sepia shots by sessile oaks,
a bluebell glade, and a swing
posted between fallen beech trees.

At Drombeg we catch the setting sun
and try to pick up clues
to a body found with smashed pottery
and shale near the *fulacht fiadh*
one snowy evening
nearly three thousand years ago.

ALBUFEIRA

I head to Praia da Falésia's reddish cliffs
set against green pine groves
and stand on a rickety wooden platform

to observe sea daffodils, Cretan trefoil, sea holly.
Young families build sandcastles,
couples stroll barefoot across the sand.

Nick has arrived. He hasn't changed much
since Sixth Form. Martha is here too.
He didn't say she was coming.

Five or six runners fight a strong wind
to pace each other round a newly laid track
before plunging into the hotel pool, laughing.

Maybe I'll look for the cavern in the Old City
at Cova do Xorino where retreating Muslims
once sought refuge as the Castle of Paderne fell.

Nick and Martha have gone to dinner
with the British ambassador.
It's too late to venture out now.

I walk to Quinta do mel past Russian athletes,
heart rate monitors strapped to bare chests,
pounding a strangely mudless cross-country course.

It's quieter. I look out across orange groves
as I write, sip farm-fresh mint tea,
eat honey and lavender ice cream.

Two shy kittens dart into the shrubs,
fixing their eyes on me from the undergrowth.
Para Além da Saudade plays softly in the background.

Runners from the camp start to appear for lunch.
They don't seem to recognise me,
but I know it's time to move on.

TOM DONALD IS A MUSICIAN OF RARE GENIUS

I speak as somebody almost uniquely
unqualified to pass judgement on musical talent.
What I know would leave white space
on the back of a second-class stamp.

Bach, The Beatles, Lady Gaga:
the scarecrow from Coonabarabran
jams them into one evening
and even, after a brief interval,
blends the sounds of el-Andaleeb el-Asmar
in a fugue, hurriedly improvised
to an insistent request (he claims):
'You'd better leave now
if you're a musical neo-con.'

His halting Aussie murmur
barely carries to the back row
of Robert Adam's neo-classical Music Room
designed for the Countess of Hell,
once a convenient bolt-hole
for the Cambridge Five
who met each week under cover
of art restoration, unaware
they were being watched
(I sit on Sir Anthony's seat
in the plush basement cloakroom
to the sound of Gregorian chanting
of Cistercian monks).

In the Music Room, middle-aged men click,
click, tap, tap, click,
to a now familiar rhythm;

implausibly pretty girls, reeled in
by the promoter, gently sway side to side
while the hay-man turns his straw-covered eyes
to the wall to shelter from the lenses of his guests.

His creased green jacket has seen action:
Dixieland gigs on the back of trucks
in small country towns;
Hackney Empire; Ronnie Scott's.
This loyal garment still struggles
to contain his coiled energy.

He leaps across the stage. Exits –
only to return to his *Blüthner* for a final trip
across centuries and continents,
as if all too aware of time,
and the man, lurking in the darkness,
who has travelled a long way,
waiting all night, just for this moment.

CHASING ELIUD KIPCHOGE

I eat pre-race breakfast too close to the start: Egyptian rice-stuffed vine leaves, florets of white asparagus dressed in mustard sauce, pistachio baklava.

A chilli competition has been set up next to the starting pens. I get as far as Naga Viper (1.4 million Scoville Heat Units) before I reach for a glass of goat's milk.

My Ethiopian pacer sits down by the side of the road. We argue violently about *The Burial of the Dead*. He refuses to move until pacified by Cat Deeley.

I stop at the 58th floor of the Wedding Cake to tie my shoelaces and sip a cup of water. Cliff Barnes insists I help him find a jewel said to have been taken from Alfred's sceptre in Winchester in 899.

I refuel at an impromptu checkpoint with baked okra cooked with tomatoes, onions and olive oil, dessert of fried rice cakes with poached greengages, chestnut mousse topped with cream and crystallised violets.

The Dalai Lama reminds me of rule 17.1.c and convinces me to go on to the finish, but it's too late to get onto the podium.

HARLEQUINADE

Once I was in a room with Andrew Jackson, Thomas More and General Gordon, and they thanked each other for various inspirations. They are all dead now. My second best idea was eating cooked spaghetti off a frisbee on a train to Dover while wearing a faux denim shirt. Sometimes I'm scared when it rains on the moor.

Here's the thing: I'm a big fan of writing poems at the dinner table, while a dead poet scribbles tart put-downs in the margins of a geology textbook, and in the shock of the moment the third daughter of the Duke of Cumberland covertly eats a custard pie.

THE AFFAIR OF THE BUNGLED TRIOLET

We're just like each other really.
Little grey cells, self-professed humility, order and method.
Find poetry and structure in the everyday, silly, grisly, guilty.
We're just like each other really.
Juggling words and images can get rather messy.
Crimes of cliché, abstraction and forced rhyme are easily detected.
We're just like each other really.
Little grey cells, self-professed humility, order and method.

BISHOPS

He slowly turns the pages of *De Republica Anglorum* and mulls over his old tutor's words. 'I would give all the books in my study for six lines of Cicero in his own hand.'

The history man looks across Great Court to the cold haunting flatness of the fens, towards London Zoo, then the Strand, then Canterbury, then Sydney. His mind glides from place to place like a fish – maybe the strange fish that slid across the Orwell in 1563, or the fish that slithered away from Moses into the sea on his way to his encounter with the verdant mystery man – until at last he reaches post-colonial Khartoum, downing litres of coffee and slinking among the dhows of pearl fishers on the Nile.

Maggie enters. She answers affable enquiries about her son's latest footballing exploits with pride, then begins dusting distractedly. This is her favourite set – unexpectedly eclectic relics of a not-unchequered past: climbing gear, fragments of a once-brightly painted Etruscan terracotta sarcophagus, rowing blades and a wooden Sigui mask.

On a bookshelf, agricultural labourers mix freely with monarchs and bishops in posthumous democracy.

Bishops, always bishops. Butter-fingered Sheppard who riled helpless bowlers watching on as precious edges spilled through the slips, who unsettled anxious parents waiting at the font; rebellious Sancroft, one of seven brothers whose protests took them to the Tower; genial Grindal, the gentle shepherd who introduced the tamarisk to England. Tutu mischievously muscles into the Cambridge conclave just in time. Djembe fills the air – had she expected Bach?

Maggie hurries out before he can explain.

Now he must keep the peace at High Table with the combustible quartet of scholars: Elton, Neale, Hill, Trevor-Roper. For just one evening, can he find a way to persuade them to put aside their faculty fireworks?

HENRY FONDA'S LUCKY HAT

I hear Jack and Sarah are wearing Marie Antoinette
and Louis XVI outfits bought in Marrakesh
on their fifth wedding anniversary.

The invite calls for '80s movie icons'
but my emblems were annual skirmishes
at the Oil Barons' Ball and Bobby emerging
from an amaranthine shower of the absurd,
so trawling '100 greatest films of the 80s' reveals:

A Connecticut Yankee in King Arthur's Court
Adventures of Buckaroo Banzai Across the 8th *Dimension*
The Man with Two Brains
Ferris Bueller's Day Off.

In case no one twigs tonight
I'm Norman Thayer
On Golden Pond.

LOCKDOWN

I'm setting fire to an air guitar
Roasted cauliflower, olive oil and chilli flakes
I'm becoming a real fan, dangerously so
Add thyme, and if you fancy, some bay
Please don't start crying
I didn't cheat
I won you lost, just accept it and move on

Adding sesame seeds is icing on the cake
A quantum physicist would probably agree
This is one of those times when it's better to be wrong
than to be a know-it-all
I'm the winner
No I'm the winner
Everyone's a winner, baby!

Pistachio, cardamom, orange and dark chocolate buns
It's so simple
I'm sunny and relaxed
I've got to run to make a repeating pattern telescope
Please don't start crying
I didn't cheat
I won you lost, just accept it and move on

I'm sulking in my room with my barometer
Jeans no longer fit
Marvin the penguin is unimpressed
that he has been overlooked
I'm the winner
No I'm the winner
Everyone's a winner, baby!

We've laminated just about everything in the house
I've been to Connemara, twice
I have an aubergine in the fridge
What's the Time, Mr Wolf?
Please don't start crying
I didn't cheat
I won you lost, just accept it and move on

A pale clouded yellow butterfly
flies across a hand-woven silk carpet
from Shiraz – or was it Whitby?
It's hard always being right
I'm the winner
No I'm the winner
Everyone's a winner, baby!

I think they're playing Grandma's Footsteps
I'm putting this up there with the day
I discovered Russian military maps of Whitstable, 1964
and learned how monkeys peel bananas
Please don't start crying
I didn't cheat
I won you lost, just accept it and move on

PHEIDIPPIDES

blast thresholds through Friday evening hail
blench in the cryotherapy chamber's last chance saloon
wake fretting at a 3 a.m. derailment on the racing line
deplete energy with a novice's fierce dance routine
flail in the slipstream of a too speedy skort
snatch Jelly Babies from high-fiving kids at Shadwell
get overtaken by a toilet at the Tower
bite frantically at a sachet of factory-fresh fruits
fight the Naseby raging inside you
clasp your battle souvenir like a venerated relic
jostle through the makeshift Renkioi
shuffle down the stairs like your great-grandfather
peel dank kit off your weeping nipples
shovel calories like you've just escaped Leningrad
start again like a trader after a market crash

WAR WIDOW

Hunched over a rusted gate,
a sharp-tongued old lady stands sentinel
every evening at precisely ten minutes past five.
I sense her distress, break off shooting practice
against the garage door and uproot a sunflower
from a scorched front lawn –
a peace offering, perhaps a bribe.
They say it's the first time
anyone has seen her smile
since her husband came back
from the field hospital at Étaples.

THREE MUSKETEERS

I console you after a first-ball duck,
celebrate your promotion, wedding, new house.
I'm always in the background,
you won't find me on TV ads or billboards
or planting my prints in Hollywood Boulevard.
I'm pretty low maintenance.
They say I'm tough to get to know,
that's just because I take a while to warm up.
I'm often mistaken for something else:
an Arabic letter, Swedish river, Cambodian village
or famous writer. I get abused from time to time,
because of my Sanskrit name, I guess.
I'm a faithful friend with many names:
mung, *urud*, *masoor*.

OLD BROMPTON ROAD

I spill a glass of water, look for the bathroom.
That's when I glimpse *Inspiration from the Sea*.
My birthday gift to Ekaterina.
She still has it after all.
'You become responsible, forever, for what you have tamed.'
Nick and Marie are sparring:
Existentialism, Suprematism, Surrealists in Egypt.
Camus was a goalkeeper, I say.
Colours seem to shift, ambiguous, darker than I imagined.
Marie reads from *Alert for the Anticolonial Conscience*.
Nick declares the *pieds noir* warriors against political correctness.
A provocative half-smile in Marie's direction.
Missed calls. A text.
Mike claims he's missed his train and decided to go home.
If only I could turn back.
'The fated victims shuddering, roll their eyes / In wild despair.'
'Rain, midnight rain, nothing but the wild rain.'

ADVICE TO MY YOUNGER SELF

Walk through the green door
Write every stop on the tube map backwards
Philosophy is on the third floor
Which road leads to the forum?
Sharpen four pencils, but the fifth…
Roundabouts will make you go round in circles
O caterpillar, why are you sleeping in fresh snow?
A circle does not smell like a square
Julius Caesar is dead
The map room is temporarily closed for refurbishments
Slice open a durian before midnight
Climb the mountain, listen to clouds laughing

FOREST RENDEZ-VOUS

On a cold February evening I cross a stone bridge
over a frozen stream to deserted woodland. Silver birch trees dance,
branches pray in howling wind. I stand for two hours or more hypnotised,
twisting fallen twigs in my hands. A woman appears, her wedding dress embroidered
with carline thistles, red belt around her waist, dark velvet crown on her head,
henna-painted hands holding a violin. It is as if she had been expecting me.

‘My name is Hiba, meaning gift from God.’
I waited all my life to be brought to this place, yet now I can’t speak.
She laughs: ‘Hope is a bitter, dangerous fruit.’
‘Must all great art come from sadness, suffering, pain?’
As light fades, a lion enters the clearing.
Hiba climbs on the lion’s back, strokes its thick dark mane.
Lion and bride disappear into the forest. I lean on the white bark
of a birch tree, and see that I have started to cry.

DAISY

I am a blue-grey pebble cast into Letcombe Brook on your fifth birthday
I am a double-decker bus hurled into the sandpit when playtime ended
I am handprints in sand at Barafundle Bay
I am a wheelchair whizzing along corridors, flying up and down hills by the ballet school
I am cherry blossom dusting daisy-covered grass
I am pink hydrangea growing by the willow tree in the Friends Forever garden
I am a swallow carrying rubies, sapphires and gold leaf, come to say goodbye
I am a nightingale piercing my breast on a rose-thorn
I am a nightlight that fills the sky with glitter-stars
I am a silver star you comfort when my tears fall to earth
I am Daisy

BEDOUIN OF THE HEART

BILAL'S FOOTSTEPS

Wa huzna, wa huzna!
If only we had not lived

to see your sparkling hazel eyes
turn dim and hollow.

Wa huzna, wa huzna,
what a fierce day of grief.

But for you a day of joy,
tonight you dine again

with your Beloved
and your fallen friends.

You dream of fresh dates,
cool running water,

a gentle breeze,
as you dreamed once before

when you were dragged through the streets,
pelted by jeering children

abusing your race,
flayed in the hot sand,

branded by hot iron rods,
wrists and ankles shackled,

your chest crushed
by a boulder that took five men to lift,

deprived of water for days
until you fell unconscious.

Your cry of defiance echoes
through centuries, unyielding

resistance to the idols men carved
with their hands, and minds,

your unflinching bond with the One
Who destroyed the army of the elephants

and opened the door to your revenge
on the day of Badr.

You were freed for ten,
our master freed by our master,

he would have paid a hundred,
or a thousand,

though as a final taunt
your perfumed tormentor

scoffed he would have accepted
even one.

After the conquest
a dazed throng watched

as you climbed above the sacred house
and called the faithful to attention.

Wa huzna, wa huzna!
If only we had not lived

to hear your deep melodious voice
turn to a rasping whisper.

We long to hear your call once more
by the banks of Al Kawthar,

to follow your footsteps, and march
behind your banner into Al Firdaws.

BURIAL AT AL BAQI'

Two men climb down a ladder, place the bodies of a woman
and baby, coffinless, wrapped in white shrouds,
in an open chamber on one side of a deep pit.

They work quickly, block the chamber,
smash some small bricks with their hands,
scatter debris in the grave and climb out.

I sip a cup of cardamom-flavoured *qahwah,*
wash down seven sweet black dates.
Dust flies everywhere.

I feel out of place among boxthorn trees,
unable to offer comfort in the darkness,
embarrassed by my tranquility.

ARABIAN MEADOWS

Loving my beautiful new store that just opened at Mecca Mall in Saudi Arabia! – Paris Hilton, 14 November 2012

Lattice balconies and riwaq arches are flattened,
vegetable sellers and cobblers forced out,
the home of the Second of Two
in the Cave of Thawr opens as a Hilton;
an eighteenth-century Ottoman fort is bulldozed
to make way for a $15 billion clock tower,
complete with seven-star hotel,
luxury penthouses more expensive
than Monaco apartments;
a gigantic shopping mall
in the shape of a tiered wedding cake,
where Paris Hilton jostles with Swarovski and La Senza,
and the house of the first Mother of the Believers
is recast as a public toilet.

BEFORE THE ADHAN

Between Ottoman pillars, a crevice cracks
open across a gap-toothed blue carpet.
The old man is missing.

I never knew his name
but each week he would smile
and whisper to his friends:

'Give the young man the *masahif*,
he'll stack them, he always does.'
Our little ritual.

A flash jacket lands on the old man's spot
like a flag planted in some imperial outpost
and a clean-shaven subaltern elbows in.

He doles out his sandalwood attar, nonchalantly
pulls a small gold-leaf *mushaf* from his pocket
and begins to read.

SONG OF THE DISTRESSED

We are afraid of pillars of blood
We are afraid of crowds of unfamiliar ghosts
We are afraid of those who walk outside the walls
We are afraid of clouds gathering in the distance
We are afraid of ants marching at night
We are afraid of thunderstorms on the horizon
We are afraid of time that seems to stop
We are afraid of time that doesn't stop
We are afraid of rainbows without colours
The old men read the *Book of Sorrow* with great dignity
We are afraid of what tomorrow brings
We are afraid of sailing across the water
When we have lost our faith
When we have forgotten how to smile
We are afraid of gifts in case we burst into tears
We are afraid of the vengeance of
One we have left behind
We are afraid of the waves of the sea
We are afraid of the waves of sound
We are afraid of the sound of red clay cracking
We are afraid of the mountain pass becoming blocked
We are afraid of forgetting
We are afraid of remembering
Our parents used to pray to their God
Our parents used to sleep under the moon
Our children used to listen to their mothers' stories
Our children used to laugh in their mothers' homes
We are afraid of being afraid

DESERT DARKNESS

I am alone, stranded
in the dark desert night.
My camel has bolted,
my guide has left me,
my shelter has blown away.
I can't read the stars.

I hear a crier calling out,
feel an icy embrace.

Weigh down my scales with wealth
I could have spent.
Ransom me with tears
I could have shed.
Quench my thirst from wells
I could have dug.

Shroud my secrets with the veil
I rebelled against.

NO TOILETS IN JANNAH

No searching for Sellotape ends in Jannah
No tangled earphones in Jannah
No queues for second class stamps in Jannah
No bitter pomegranate pips in Jannah
No blocked drains in Jannah
No darning in Jannah
No cancelled trains in Jannah
No buffering in Jannah
No bruised apples in Jannah
No peeling onions in Jannah
No laptop reboots in Jannah
No potholes in Jannah
No crushed soggy digestives in Jannah
No toilets in Jannah

RAMADAN DIARY

This is a month of revelation unveiled in the cave of Hira
launching a global reformation twelve years before Hijra.

This is a month of scorching heat, long days, short nights,
a shield to put a malefic enemy to flight.

This is a month of struggle, long runs under a searing sun
craving raspberry ripple or a blast from a water gun.

This is a month of charity – share a meal, *fattoush*, *tajine*,
slake a cat's thirst, forgive a debt, offer half a date or clementine.

This is a month of celebration, fire crackers, *kanafeh* and kites, rice and *bettifour*,
lanterns, the beat of the *bedug*, henna and candles, popcorn and sugar.

This is a month of mercy and renewal, dance with the dervishes,
seek the Night of Decree, all else perishes.

IRON-BREAST

I was born in No Man's Land
among pines, birch, maple, poplar.

As a boy I hunted white-tailed deer and partridge,
fished for blueheads, sunfish, northern pike,

and gathered buckets of huckleberries,
until I ran away to Clown Alley

to live with animal trainers, acrobats,
roustabouts, and tuba players,

a panther, two gorillas,
a twelve-foot boa constrictor

and Minyak the elephant.
The Sioux named me 'Iron-breast'.

My broken nose took me to the sands of
Beni Youssef and Abu Ruwash.

I've been cardinal, sculptor, knight, king,
general, prophet, slave, conductor,

quarterback, astronaut,
lean and volcanic Old Hickory.

I fought for liberty on the steps
of the Lincoln Memorial

and in Charlotte waving
an ancient musket above my head.

When these hands are cold,
and dead, bury my body

where I once triumphed,
in the Great Circus of Antioch.

DAUGHTER OF THE DESERT

Where are you now?

In my office in Baghdad. It's by the river and wonderfully cool. I have a writing table, a sofa, some chairs and rugs, a couple of old Persian glass vases, and maps. Maps are my passion. Outside reeks of antiquity and is so thick with the dust of ages that you can't see through it.

You are fluent in several languages. Do you find it easy to learn a new language?

Arabic was very hard at first – did you know there are five words for 'wall' and 36 ways of forming the plural?

What would you say is your greatest achievement?

The Archaeological Museum in Baghdad. I wanted to help preserve Iraqi culture and history – we managed to secure some important relics for the museum. And I would have to say my books, especially *The Palace and Mosque at Ukhaidir* and *Review of the Civil Administration of Mesopotamia*.

Tell us about Henry Cadogan – you were engaged, weren't you?

Henry loved a flutter. He was tall and red and very thin. A great sportsman, devoted to riding, though he couldn't ride in the least. And a lover of Hafez, like myself. One morning we visited the Citadel of the Dead and climbed the Tower of Silence. A year later Henry fell into an icy river while fishing and died of pneumonia.

And Charles Doughty-Wylie?
I was very fond of Dick (as his friends called him) and his pleasant little wife. He called me his 'queen of the desert'. As he wrote to me once, 'the subtle book eludes, but our hands met on the cover.' Sadly, Dick died at Gallipoli.

You were the first woman to win a first class degree in modern history at Oxford, the first woman officer in the history of British intelligence and the only woman present at the Cairo Conference. Do you consider yourself a feminist?
Certainly not! I don't agree with votes for women at all. In fact, I was at one time a member of the Anti-Suffrage League.

Didn't you once say that 'one can't do much more than sit and record if one is of my sex, devil take it'?
That remark was taken out of context.

You said T.E. Lawrence 'could ignite fires in cold rooms'. Did you get on well?
Yes, I first met him at the dig at Carchemish. We were similar in many ways. Neither of us suffered fools gladly, for a start. When we worked together in Cairo we made vast schemes for the government of the universe. Everyone knows he could be volatile though: when he stormed out of the Paris peace conference he pinned his *Croix de Guerre* to a dog's collar!

Have you ever felt in danger?
Yes, I once survived by clinging to a rock face for 53 hours on the unclimbed north-east face of the Finsteraarhorn when my expedition was caught in a blizzard. When things are as bad as ever they can be you cease to mind them much. You set your teeth and battle with the fates. And I always sleep with a gun under my pillow.

How would you like to be remembered?
As 'Al Khatun'. A 'daughter of the desert', as the Bedouins of the Bani Sakhr tribe call me. I'm immensely proud of that.

DESERT PILGRIM

Barefoot, thirsty, I tread on hot marble,
anti-clockwise,
in forty-five-degree heat.

I cling to the *kiswah*
in the midday sun, almost sick
from sweat and stench

and occasional fights.
Northern Line in rush hour
seems like a beach in winter

but at last I reach the Black Stone
to kiss the rock that, it is said, fell to Earth
dazzling white before we stained it.

I scurry between two hills,
a mother foraging for water
in the desert.

I shave my head,
pay extra for an efficient barber,
fresh blade, no nicks.

A young man from Ha'il
sheepishly draws geometric patterns
on a dark green carpet,

says Dammam derives its name
from the sound of drums
to announce hunting season.

I soothe sore blistered feet
at dusk, munch *za'atar*-dipped bread,
gulp sweet mint tea.

KONYA

I’m ready for you to arrive at any moment.
I offer comfort, stars and lamps to navigate
your way across a narrow bridge,
comb and pitcher to scour off grime,
a furnace to extract silver from dross.
As Rumi says from his turquoise tomb,
‘Come, even if you’ve broken your vows
a hundred times’ you’re welcome,
share a pot of sweet tea, mangoes,
watermelon, listen to the reed flute play,
‘what you seek is seeking you.’

SANDSTORM

In the shade of an acacia tree, I pray like Moses by the well of Midian,
waiting for a Yemeni caravan heavy with spices and gold.

Once in a dream I saw you tend sheep and goats,
fetch water for a stray dog, pull a thorn from the foot of a horse.

Why did you raid my green heart? I offered you red camels,
wrote a *qasidah* to rival the *Mu'allaqa* of Imru' al-Qays,

built a walled retreat of fountains, planted tulips, roses,
rows of pomegranate and cypress trees embracing.

Yet still I move across the desert of Rub' al-Khali,
fight bitter *haboob* winds, hunt wild oryx.

I am a Bedouin of the heart. I pitch my tent by a raging fire
which cannot last, sit alone under the moon and stars.

NOTES ON POEMS

The notes below provide some further background which may interest the reader and provide a different perspective to the poems. I have included references to key source material (e.g. quotations included in the text of a poem, or an important source of inspiration). I have also provided explanations for some information that might otherwise be hard to find.

1. 'Witnesses': Sumayyah and her husband Yasir are generally regarded as the first martyrs in Islam. 'Al-Kawthar' (meaning 'abundance') refers to a river in Paradise.

2. 'Bibi, Are You Living?': Anarkali was the nickname of a courtesan said to be the lover of the 16th century Mughal prince Salim (later to become Emperor Jahangir). A 1960 Bollywood epic *Mughal-e-Azam* (or *The Great Mughal*) was based on the legend of Salim and Anarkali. This film, for many years the highest grossing Indian film, featured Dilip Kumar (the 'Bollywood tragedy king', born Muhammad Yusuf Khan in 1922) and Madhubala (a famous Indian actress, 1933-1969) in the lead roles. The 'knighted poet of the East' refers to Muhammad Iqbal (1877-1938).

'Layla and Majnun' is an ancient Arabic legend about the ill-fated love of a young man Qays (nicknamed 'Majnun', or 'madman') and a beautiful young woman named Layla.

3. 'Last Words': Source material from William B. Brahms, *Last Words of Notable People* (Reference Desk Press, 2010).

4. ‘Yellow Rose’: Hafez (also spelled Hafiz) refers to the 14th century Persian poet Shams al-Din Muhammad Hafez from Shiraz, in modern day Iran.

5. ‘Ashes’: The mortician’s name, Moat, is similar to the Arabic for death (*al Mawt*).

6. ‘Double Latin’: The ‘Freemantle Doctor’ is a cooling afternoon sea breeze that occurs during summer months in Western Australia. It is said to have had an impact on cricket matches at the WACA ground in Perth, where Test matches took place between 1970 and 2017.

7. ‘Looking for Louisa’: This poem was inspired by a visit to Dorset in 2017. The visit took in Dorchester, Higher Bockhampton and Max Gate (all associated with Thomas Hardy), as well as Lyme Regis. 150 years earlier, in 1867, Alfred Lord Tennyson visited Lyme Regis to find the spot on The Cobb where Louisa Musgrove, a character in Jane Austen’s *Persuasion,* had fallen.

8. ‘Persian Rose’: The following lines are taken from Milton’s *Samson Agonistes:*
‘…apt words have power to swage / The tumours of a troubl’d mind, / And are as balm to fester’d wounds’ (lines 184-186)
‘…Imprison’d…/ shut up from outward light…’ (lines 158 and 160)

9. ‘A Birthday Poem’ was written to celebrate a 70th birthday in 2018.

10. ‘Baked Alaska’: ‘Hot flesh and cold hearts’ is from Matthea Harvey’s poem ‘Baked Alaska, a Theory of’.

‘Orange Pekoe’ is a tearoom in Barnes, South West London. (It also refers to the highest grade of Western and South Asian black teas).

‘Master Blaster’ and ‘Whispering Death’ are nicknames of two famous West Indian cricketers, Sir Viv Richards and Michael Holding.

11. ‘The Last Ride’: ‘Hardy’ and ‘Bronte’ are two hospital wards. ‘Zamzam’ is water from a well in Masjid al-Haram in Makkah in present day Saudi Arabia. Muslims believe that water originally appeared there when Ismail (Ishmael) was thirsty and his mother Hajar (Hagar) was desperately searching for water in the desert. Millions of pilgrims drink from this well every year, and believe it to have many health benefits.

12. ‘Flower of Kent’: ‘Flower of Kent’ is a large culinary apple. It is identical to the variety growing in Isaac Newton’s garden at Woolsthorpe Manor, near Grantham in Lincolnshire. According to legend, Newton was sitting under this tree when an apple fell to the ground, leading to him developing his theory of gravitation. The original Isaac Newton tree died in 1814, but trees descending from it by grafting still survive today.

13. ‘Merton Priory’: During the Saxon period the first documentary evidence for Merton appears. Merton as a place name can be traced to as early as the 7th century, supporting the likelihood of settlement by that date. It is usually translated as ‘the farm by the pond’ or alternatively as ‘Maera’s homestead’. (Source: https://www.mertonpriory.org/history/)

'Embrothering': Dr. Cox, in his *English Monasteries*, quotes the report of the commissioners for dissolving the Austin priory of Ulverscroft, which says that the canons were engaged in 'embrothering (illuminating) or writing books in a very fair hand; making their own garments, carving, painting, and graffing; the house keeping such hospitality that except by singular good provision it would not be maintained; and the relief of the poor inhabitants.' (Source: https://www.british-history.ac.uk/st-barts-records/vol1/pp19-34)

14. 'Maiden Queen' was written in response to *Lady on a Chair*, a painting by Cheryl Tarbuck, exhibited at the *Memory* exhibition in London in 2019.

15. 'Who Stole The Hymn Books?': This poem was inspired by a ride on the number 15 Routemaster bus and a subsequent stroll around Covent Garden.

According to John Stowe, 'candlewright' is a 'maker of candles', from which Cannon Street got its name.

16. 'Seven Days in Richmond': This poem was written in response to *Staggered*, a painting by Sue Bunn, displayed at the *Memory* exhibition in London in 2019.

17. 'Honeymoon': The Lanesborough Hotel in Hyde Park was formerly St George's Hospital, until the hospital moved to its present site in Tooting. The contrast between an $18^{th}/19^{th}$ century hospital (the hospital opened in 1733) and a modern luxury hotel seemed intriguing. William Wilkins, the architect of the original St George's Hospital, also designed my old college, Downing College, Cambridge.

18: 'Earth, Rock, Sea': In 2017, I travelled to Ireland and, with a small group of friends, visited a number of locations referenced in the poem – including Blarney Castle, Bere Island, Barleycove, Mizen Head, Skibbereen, Lough Hyne and Drombeg.

19. 'Tom Donald Is A Musician Of Rare Genius': Tom Donald is an Australian piano virtuoso with classical roots, which he mixes with a strong interest in styles including Latin, folk, soul, rock and jazz. He is the founder of the London Contemporary School of Piano. I am grateful to David Frost for inviting me to a Tom Donald event at Home House in Portman Square, London, which inspired this poem.

20. 'Harlequinade' is a collage poem, combining original material and text from the following poems:

Crispin Best, 'poem at the dinner table' and 'some mornings'
Daisy Lafarge, 'mineral intimacy'
Mary Ruefle, '2015'

21. 'The Affair of the Bungled Triolet' was inspired by Agatha Christie's fictional Belgian detective Hercule Poirot.

22. 'Bishops' was inspired by Patrick Collinson, Regius Professor of Modern History at the University of Cambridge (1988-96). Further source material was taken from his book, *The History of a History Man* (Boydell Press, 2011).

23. 'Lockdown': the text in this poem was taken from a Microsoft Teams channel at work. I am grateful to colleagues for providing the source material.

24. 'Old Brompton Road' was written in response to a series of paintings by Eva Vazaka, displayed at the *Memory* exhibition in London in 2019.

Inspiration from the Sea is a 1963 oil painting by Ramses Younan.

'You become responsible, forever, for what you have tamed' is taken from Antoine de Saint-Exupéry, *The Little Prince* (1943).

'Alert for the Anticolonial Conscience' was a petition circulated in Algeria in 2010, on the 50th anniversary of Albert Camus' death. Its proponents criticised attempts to mark the anniversary (Source: https://www.theguardian.com/books/2010/feb/28/albert-camus-algeria-anniversary-row)

'The fated victims shuddering roll their eyes / In wild despair' is taken from William Falconer's poem, 'The Shipwreck' (first published in 1762).

'Rain, midnight rain, nothing but the wild rain' is taken from Edward Thomas' poem 'Rain' (1916).

25. 'Daisy' was inspired by Stephanie Nimmo, *Goodbye Daisy* (Hashtag Press, 2019). References to the swallow and nightingale are to 'The Happy Prince', and 'The Nightingale and the Rose', children's stories written by Oscar Wilde (first published in 1888).

26. 'Bilal's Footsteps': 'Bilal's Footsteps' references the Hadith (saying of the Prophet Muhammad peace be upon him): 'I heard your footsteps in front of me in Paradise,' (Sahih al-Bukhari, Hadith number 1149). Bilal ibn Rabah was one of the earliest converts to Islam, and was tortured in the hot desert sun before he was eventually freed. He became the muezzin (caller to prayer), and was the first to make the call to prayer in the three holiest mosques in Islam in Makkah, Madinah and Jerusalem.

'*Wa huzna*' is an Arabic expression meaning 'what grief!' 'Al Firdaws' refers to the highest section of Paradise.

27. 'Burial at Al Baqi': this poem, like 'Arabian Meadows' and 'Desert Pilgrim', was inspired by trips to Makkah and Madinah for Hajj and Umrah. Burials that take place in Al Baqi' in Madinah by lamplight after the early morning prayer are particularly atmospheric.

28. 'Arabian Meadows': 'Second of Two in the Cave of Thawr' refers to Abu Bakr who hid in a cave with the Prophet Muhammad peace be upon him when they were migrating from Makkah to Madinah to escape persecution.

This poem uses source material from a number of articles about the changing landscape of Makkah (e.g. https://time.com/3584585/saudi-arabia-bulldozes-over-its-heritage/)

29. 'Before the *Adhan*': '*mushaf*' (pl. '*masahif*') refers to a written copy of the Qur'an.

30. 'Song of the Distressed' was inspired by Immanuel Mifsud's Maltese-language poem 'Il-Kantiku tad-Dipressi' ('Canticle of the Depressed').

31. 'Ramadan Diary': '*bettifour*' (from the French '*petit four*') are dry baked goods including biscuits, baked meringues and macaroons served in Sudan during Eid al-Fitr celebrations at the end of the month of Ramadan.

32. 'Iron-breast' was inspired by Charlton Heston, *In The Arena: the Autobiography* (Harper Collins, 1995).

33. 'Daughter of the Desert': My interest in Gertude Bell was originally sparked by a conversation with Dr Susan Bayly, Professor of Historical Anthropology at Cambridge University and Fellow of Christ's College, Cambridge. Further inspiration for this poem came from Georgina Howell, *Queen of the Desert: The Extraordinary Life of Gertrude Bell* (Pan Books, 2007). The form of this poem was inspired by the '60 Seconds' series of interviews in London's *Metro* newspaper.

34. 'Desert Pilgrim': '*kiswah*' is the black brocade cloth covering the Kaaba in Makkah.

35. 'Konya': quotes in this poem are attributed to the 13th century Persian poet Jalal ad-Din Muhammad Rumi.

36. 'Sandstorm' was displayed with a series of sculptures by Rula Sayegh for the *Memory* exhibition in London in 2019.

Imru' al-Qays is acknowledged as the most distinguished pre-Islamic Arab poet. He was the author of one of the seven odes (*qasidahs*) in the famed collection of pre-Islamic poetry called *Al-Mu'allaqat* (sing. *Mu'allaqa*).

ACKNOWLEDGEMENTS

I am grateful to editors of the following poetry magazines and journals for publishing earlier versions of several poems in this collection: *Amaryllis, British Life in Poetry, Envoi, Ink, Sweat & Tears, Orbis, Porridge, Snakeskin, The Interpreter's House, Under the Radar.*

Some poems in this collection previously appeared in *'Bibi, Are You Living?'* (Eyewear, 2017), and *Memory,* a full-colour, limited-edition book published to accompany an exhibition of poetry and art held in conjunction with The Art Cooperative at the Menier Gallery in London in 2019. Thank you to Sue Bunn and other members of The Art Cooperative for inviting me to work with them on the *Memory* exhibition, an enjoyable collaboration I hope we can repeat in future.

I would like to thank Dr Todd Swift and the Eyewear Publishing team for agreeing to follow up my 2017 pamphlet by publishing this book. In particular thank you to my editor Cate Myddleton-Evans for making many helpful suggestions during editing and production.

I have benefited from advice and encouragement from a number of poets. Simon Barraclough in particular was an early mentor. Others who have kindly commented on versions of many poems in this collection include Kayo Chingonyi, Katy Evans-Bush, Emma Hammond, Helen Mort, Pascale Petit, Maurice Riordan, Richard Scott and Jane Yeh. Of course none of them are to blame for any of my poems missing their mark.

Many family members, friends and colleagues have sparked poems in this collection, either by sharing stories or providing inspiration in other ways. A big thank you to all of you, and to everyone who has read my poems, shared your feedback and provided encouragement and support.

I very much hope you enjoy reading the poems in this book, and would love to hear from you if you have any comments on the collection.

Lightning Source UK Ltd.
Milton Keynes UK
UKHW010742031221
394996UK00001B/28

9 781913 606749